The

An IT novel demonstrating the work and life challenges of a young professional woman aiming to become a world-class leader.

For the rising young leaders in Technology and Engineering, this story is for you.

Lessons Learned about IT, leadership skills, Service Management, Lean, Agile, Outsourcing, IT Incident and Crisis Management, and Team Management.

Anastral Rusten

ISBN: 978-1-917007-60-3

First edition 2023.

Disclaimer

This is a work of fiction. Names, characters, business, events, and incidents are the products of the author's imagination. Any resemblance to actual persons, living or dead, or actual events is purely coincidental.

Acknowledgements

I would like to thank many of my colleagues who have read this book and provided me with their feedback.

The person also responsible for making this book a reality is my husband, Eddie - my partner in marriage, business, and in life. Thank you.

Contents

INTRODUCTION

Catherine Saab is an IT Infrastructure Operations Manager who has found her dream job at CRN Design. She started her job by getting to know the team and her colleagues. Catherine was promised work-life balance, women equal opportunities, and every Friday afternoon off in the new job. In this story, Catherine takes us on her work journey as she describes her challenges and surprises at the new job. Also, she sets out some lessons to young and future leaders on IT, team management, service management, six sigma, process improvement, DevOps, and ITIL.

CHAPTER 1
THE DREAM JOB

"My dream job has already happened."

~ Kathleen Quinlan

Every now and then, I go on LinkedIn and check job openings to see what jobs are highly requested in my domain and check what certifications I need to stay up to date with the job market. One day, while I was reading the job description on the internet, a few keywords attracted me to this IT Infrastructure Operations Manager position at *CRN Design* Inc. So, I found myself clicking on the apply button. Words just stood out for me in the job description, like "every Friday afternoon off...manage onsite and virtual IT teams across Canada...work with new technology...work-life balance...Women Equality." All these items are important working conditions that were missing at my current job.

A few days later, I received an email requesting an interview.

Dressed in a black suit, I opened the entrance door of the building tower of *CRN Design Inc.* I was amazed by the granite, luxurious architecture of the 20th-floor building. So, I took the elevator to the 5th floor, and when the elevator's door opened, there were a bunch of people gathered around in a circle arguing about a technical issue.

Slowly, a man turned around and looked at me with a puzzled face. I promptly said, "I am here for the IT Infrastructure Operations Manager interview." He replied with a smile, "I will be with you in a second. Please go to the conference room and wait for me."

My eyes became wide open. I just realized that that man standing in front of me was the IT Infrastructure Director - Richard Martin - my future boss if hired.

Richard was a tall, skinny man wearing a black shirt and black pants. With a gentle smile, Richard entered the office and shook my hand *(I already liked this guy... he seemed like a gentleman, I said to myself).*

"My name is Richard." His eyes squinted as he sat across the table. He looked very young, but as I looked at his wrinkled neck, I could notice that he was way older than me...maybe he was in his late 50s.

Richard started waving his pen and asked, “Was it hard to find the place?” *(I thought to myself: Why do they always start with this question... I know it is an icebreaker, but it is the same question I always get asked at every interview).* I replied with a smile, “No, it was not hard. I have worked for ten years in this downtown. I know the place very well.” Then, he smiled while saying, “Let’s start by telling me about yourself.”

I nodded and with confidence and said:

“As you know from my CV, my name is Catherine Saab. I am an IT Cloud and Operations manager. At my current work, I manage two datacenters and twelve people, including network, database, and windows system engineers. I have over 15 years of experience in IT. I rolled out ITSM and ERP software in my previous position and handled servers & data migration projects for around fifty 50 clients. Moreover, I created processes and procedures that enabled my current company to obtain a SOC compliance report. The Security Operation Center (SOC) report helped my company to continuously monitor and improve our security. We were able to prevent, detect, analyze, and respond to cybersecurity incidents faster after SOC. As for my education, I have a master's degree in software engineering. Also, I hold multiple certifications."

He put his pen down and asked, "Did you manage a private or public cloud?"

"Private," I answered with confidence. He gave me a disgusted smile. *(I was surprised.)*

Then, he went on to ask, "What controls do you have over Private Cloud versus Public Cloud?"

"Security… more control because it is your own infrastructure," I replied.

"I assume you have backups. *(I nodded)* How do you ensure your team is always checking the backups?"

"I have my team on a rotational schedule to check the backups. There is a file on SharePoint that they must sign off upon verifying the success of the backup. If the backup fails, they open a ticket and ensure it is fixed."

"How many servers are you and your team responsible for at your current work?" Richard asked.

"1200 servers, and we replicate our critical services to our disaster recovery (DR) data center.

Our main data center is in Montreal, and we have another one in Florida," I replied.

Richard continued with his questions, "Do you do disaster recovery tests?"

"Yes, every quarter," I said.

"Now, if it does not bother you, I will invite our technical operations team leader to join us in the interview. His name is Ronald." Richard said. *(I nodded)*

A tall, bold man with a big dragon tattoo on his arm stepped into the conference room. He entered and greeted me with a smile. From his questions, I concluded that Ronald was more concerned about my management style. He asked me about my way of managing the staff.

I told him that I do not like to micromanage my team. Members of my third-level support team are supposed to be professionals, and if they are not, then I will micromanage. Usually, I hold my team members accountable for their work. To ensure work is progressing, I hold daily scrum meetings and ensure all members are well-aligned with their tasks. My approach is to use Kanban to keep up with tasks. Kanban is a popular framework used to implement agile and DevOps. It enables the team to communicate their work capacity. Work items are usually represented visually on a virtual Kanban Board, allowing my team members to see the state of every piece of work at any time.

Ronald smiled and seemed to be happy with my answer.

Richard stood up and started walking around.

He said, "CRN Design is a global industrial company with headquarters in Seattle, Washington. This company has 10,000 employees in Canada. At CRN Design Canada, we have 2 data centers – the main data center is in Montreal, and the DR datacenter is in Toronto. We have plans to move our servers to the public cloud. But before doing so, we must quantify our IT assets and stabilize the services running in our Montreal data center."

Richard then sat down, and while tapping his fingers on the table, he continued, "The job of the new IT Operations manager is to establish IT processes, manage a team of 15 people, mostly all virtual team, ensure maintenance of our IT infrastructure, and provide service delivery to the employees of *CRN Design Canada*."

"May I ask a question? I interrupted. *(He nodded in acceptance)*

"Do you have a tool to patch your servers, or how do you patch your servers?"

Richard replied that they need to establish a process for patching. *(I was surprised with the answer).* Then, I asked, "How long have you been in this company? And do you like working here?"

He replied with a smile, "I have been working at *CRN Design* for four years, and yes, I like working here. I have the freedom to make a lot of changes."

Employee's engagement is gained when employees are given the capability and freedom to do changes. This creates loyalty, happiness, and sense of belonging to the organization. The result is a happy and productive work force with a positive culture.

When I left the office, Richard was kind enough to walk me to the elevator. So, I stood still, and with a smile, I shook his hand goodbye.

As I got out of the building, I couldn't help but notice the beautiful weather that day. The sky was blue, and there was barely any cloud. Taking a promenade along Sherbrooke Street in downtown Montreal, I was observing the tall green trees dancing along with the wind. I enjoyed viewing people happily dining on the terrasses of the restaurants and kids enjoying their colorful ice creams.

Then, I decided to hike towards Mount Royal, Montreal's highest point of the city overlooking the St. Lawrence River and the city of Montreal. The view of this green oasis that comprises 494 hectares of forest and trails was spectacular. I was enjoying the beautiful scenery of people paddling in their canoes in the lake and kids feeding the ducks.

Montreal is a very beautiful city!

Montreal is a unique city with fascinating architecture and history. It has a mixture taste of Europe and North America.

I really felt great that day.

My thoughts kept bringing me back to the interview. Even though I had positive vibes about the interview, I was not sure what impression I had left on Richard and Ronald. I waited patiently for their response.

A few days later, I received the job offer, and I happily accepted.

CHAPTER 2

THE TEAM

"Take time to get to know people. Understand where they are coming from, what is important to them. Make sure they are with you."

~ Jack Welch

It's my first day at the new job.

Richard greeted me in the morning and walked me to my cubicle. It was small and tidy. I was hopeful to get a private office like I had in my previous job, but I did not mind sitting close to Ronald, my technical team lead. On the other side of my cubicle was the security manager, Chris Dubey.

As Richard was introducing me to the team on the floor, he started with Chris.

"Hey Chris, I would like you to meet Catherine, our new IT Infrastructure Operations Manager."

"Nice to meet you, Catherine. We will be working a lot together. There is so much work here at CRN Design," Chris stated.

I nodded and smiled back, "Nice to meet you, Chris, and looking forward to working with you."

On the opposite side of my cubicle was Mary Martin, the IT Change Manager.

Mary greeted me warmly. She was a loud and bubbly person with cheeks as red as a tomato. She told me she was originally from Texas, USA, and moved recently to Montreal. With enthusiasm, she asked to have a meeting with me later so she could explain all about the company's IT change management process. With a smile, I requested Mary to schedule that meeting.

Then, Richard called me to his office. He provided details about my team members, explaining their strengths and weaknesses. He identified three individuals - Sandra, Valerie, and Raghu - who had poor performance. Moreover, he was planning on letting them go. Immediately, I requested to be granted some time so I could evaluate those three individuals before making any decision. Richard nodded in agreement.

So, back at my desk, I started scheduling one-on-one meetings with each member of my team. Most of my team members were in different offices across Canada. I had only three members of my team in the Montreal office.

The objective of the first one-on-one meeting - which I titled *Meet & Greet* - was to introduce myself, explain my management style, and listen to my team's concerns, challenges, and recommendations.

Having team meetings provides insight into current and future work and aligns the team's work. Those team meetings create a closely bonded team. This bonded team will then work efficiently together on increasing profits and achieving the company's objectives.

Lessons Learned:

Create team meetings and set objectives. Make sure your bonded team will work closely together on achieving the company's goals.

Most of my team members were curious to know my expectations of them and my level of flexibility. They asked questions like if they needed to be late or had a medical appointment someday and how I would like to be notified. They were happy to hear that those details did not matter to me if their work was completed on time and with quality.

Additionally, I explained to them that I valued communication and transparency. I would like to be the first to be notified about issues and projects related to my team.

We are often surprised by projects failing, budgets running out, and goals not being met late in the project simply due to a lack of communication. At work, everyone hates such surprises, especially management.

Lessons Learned:

Value communication and transparency. Make sure to continuously update management with your work to avoid surprises.

One of my objectives from the one-on-one team

meetings is to understand the current established processes and challenges. Knowing how the team is currently functioning is essential before making any change or recommendation. As I met with each of my team members, I started challenging the current status quo by asking why five times.

Just to note, "Why" is a six-sigma simple but effective method of analyzing and solving problems. By asking "why" as many times as needed, we can identify the reason a task is done a certain way and determine the root cause. This approach is used in tandem with Cause-and-Effect and Fishbone Diagrams.

My meeting with Ronald was special. I still remember he said, "I have been at the company for over twenty-five years. I was hired by the first CIO of this company. A few months ago, they promoted me from technical lead to IT Infrastructure Operations manager - your position, Catherine - but the CIO kept criticizing my work in every meeting, so I told Richard that I did not want this promotion."

He continued explaining, "Our CIO is new – he has been with us for only one year. The small engineering company that I was part of bought this big global company, *CRN Design*. As a result of the merging and acquisition, we had a young, dynamic CIO whom we all liked, then with the new company came the new CIO."

"What happened to the old CIO?" – I anxiously asked.

"They gave him an IT Director position instead of keeping his CIO position, but he did not accept and moved to another company."

"Wow!" I was shocked by this news. Then, I requested to know more about the new CIO.

Ronald said, "The new CIO… I don't know. He does not interact with us much. If he is ever in our Montreal office, he never comes to greet us (his regular IT employees). Only when there is an issue we hear from him. His name is Francisco Sanchez."

Hmmm… The new CIO is not nice and maybe arrogant - I said to myself.

Then, I wanted to make a joke with Ronald, so I asked him, "Do you know what CIO stands for?"

He said, "Chief Information Officer."

I replied, "No, Career Is Over!" We started laughing out loud.

Next, I asked him if he had any kids.

He said he had a wife and three stepchildren: A 25-year-old son named Paul, a 20-year-old daughter named Lana, and a 15-year-old daughter named Andrea. Then, he asked me the same question, so I told him I had two kids: Annie – a 14-year-old girl, and Joey – a 10-year-old boy.

The average office worker spends 28% of their work week on emails. Not surprisingly, much of this time isn't productive. Some of these emails may be urgent. Others can be dealt with in time. Unfortunately, without proper email management, inboxes can easily become a disaster.

Lessons Learned:

Organize your email inbox to properly manage your work and save time. Set rules, flag urgent emails, input precise email subjects, and set your outlook email as conversation.

As I was checking my emails, I had around 150 emails already on my first day. And every hour, I was receiving around 20 emails. Crazy! One of the first things that I did was to sort my emails in conversations so I could better manage my Outlook. Also, I created a few folders to properly categorize my projects, To-Do tasks, and team-related messages. In addition, I created rules in outlook to flag notifications coming from upper management with high importance.

As I was checking my emails closely, a meeting request from Marc Anderson, the IT Infrastructure Project Manager, grabbed my attention. Richard told me that my team works closely with Marc's team. My team supports the current infrastructure and helps Marc with the new deployments.

It was the end of my first day. What a long day, I said to myself! I barely remember the names of any of the people I met. I was a bit confused about who did what as well. My head felt so heavy! Questioning myself if I had understood the challenges that were explained to me, I felt my frustration was being elevated. I was wondering if I was going to succeed in this new job or not.

The second day, early in the morning, I took the subway and excitedly headed back to work. On the subway, enjoying my quiet time alone, I was digesting the information as I was reading Isaac Sacolick's book *Driving Digital: The Leader's Guide to Business Transformation Through Technology*. Every month, I must read at least one book to stay up to date with technology and increase my knowledge.

When I arrived at work, my first meeting was scheduled with Marc. Marc told me he was a manager working for the global company before the merge. His team was occupied with the execution of IT projects such as domain migrations from the merging and acquisitions, an evergreening project to replace old servers, security rollout, a QoS project (Quality of Service), a Cloud migration project, and Microsoft Teams deployment. He told me he really needed my team's help in accomplishing his projects.

My request to Marc was to see his project portfolio along with his project plans. He quickly sent the documents via email. I was happy to see he was well organized. All his project plans had timelines, milestones, and assigned resources. In my mind, I was gathering information about this work to try to assess the IT Infrastructure maturity level according to the capability maturity model.

I remember that following Marc's meeting, I had my first one-on-one meeting with Sandra. Sandra was working in Alberta. She seemed young and sweet in her phone conversation. She explained, "For the past three years, I have been working on backups. I took sick leave for three months, and then upon my return, I started feeling the stress crawling back upon me. The company flew me to Montreal for two months, but I don't know. I am still not happy." Trying to bond with her, I asked her if she had any kids.

Sandra replied with a giggle, "I don't even have a boyfriend!" I laughed out loud and said, "Why not get one? You seem young. *(I stopped for 2 seconds, then I continued.)* As for work, I will see what I can do for you. Give me a couple of days, and I will get back to you."

She responded with a low voice, "Thank you! Thanks for listening to me." I replied, "You are welcome. Feel free to contact me whenever you want."

I hung up the phone and headed to Richard's office, feeling upset.

Richard was buried in a pile of papers and had his glasses on. He looked up and said, "What's up?"

"I just hung up my one-on-one meeting with Sandra. She told me she can do more! She is bored and sick from doing the same job repeatedly. Please, I want her to participate in several projects besides the backups."

Richard rolled his eyes and said, “We tried putting her on projects, but she is always complaining.”

“Can I get your OK to handle this my way? She has experience in server and application support. I want to put her on the Teams rollout project and cloud migration project.” - I exclaimed.

For a second, I couldn’t read any expression on Richard’s face. Then, he said, “Ok. But keep me updated on her performance.”

I nodded in agreement and headed to my cubicle.

It was our first scrum team meeting, and I noticed Raghu did not attend the meeting. Raghu was one of my team members who Richard said to work closely with to improve his performance. Later that day, Raghu sent an email that he was sick.

So, overall, I had three of my team members in Montreal, and the rest of my team were across Canada. We had to book our daily scrum meeting at 11 am to accommodate the time zones.

Luckily, my next meeting was with Valerie. I went to meet Valerie face-to-face in the conference room as she was with me in Montreal’s office. Valerie took care of our exchange servers, investigated issues, and executed server migration projects. What I heard about Valerie was that she used to spend her time on social media. People were passing by her desk and could see she was always logged on Facebook and Instagram.

Lessons Learned:

Go the extra mile to distinguish yourself from your colleagues. This is an opportunity to stand out and get recognized for future work opportunities.

Do an extra hour a day or work on a task outside of your job description. This demonstrates that you add value to the company and make you distinguished among your colleagues.

When Valerie entered the conference room, she seemed to be in her mid-50s. She told me she had worked for three years at the company, and she is unhappy as she does tasks that are not part of her job description. I asked Valerie gently if she could avoid going on social media during working hours and emphasized that any extra effort and time she puts into the work, even if it is outside her job description, is well recognized by upper management. I continued by saying that we must always distinguish ourselves from our colleagues if we are seeking recognition, appreciation, and promotion.

As I was talking with Ronald, I was surprised that *CRN Design* does not offer coffee or beverages to its employees. By the way, I love coffee! So, I approached Richard and convinced him to purchase us a vending coffee machine instead of continuously bringing our coffee with us from home. I told him providing coffee to the employees has been proven to boost our morale and increase productivity. I assured him that soon enough, he would see great positive change in this department of *CRN Design* due to this new coffee machine. Richard was not fully convinced of the benefits of the coffee machine idea, but I felt he wanted to give it a try. I even heard him on the phone talking about me. He said, "You can't believe this! She convinced me to bring a new coffee vending machine to the office!"

I read somewhere that the average office worker drinks about 1,000 cups of coffee annually. Workers who drink it are often more productive. It improves reaction times and your ability to multitask. Coffee drinking also improves your memory and the general functions of your brain.

As I was sipping my morning coffee at my desk, an outlook meeting reminder popped up. It was a meeting with Mary, the IT Change Manager.

Mary was a structured and process-oriented change manager. She took her time to explain to me the change management process.

She said, “Every week, the IT team meets in a Technical Review Board (TRB) meeting where changes are discussed technically and formally created in the ITSM (IT Service Management) system as a change request. Change requests must be identified as normal, standard, or emergency. And for each change request, there must be a documented change plan, backout procedure, test plan, communication plan, post-implementation plan, risk, and impact assessment.”

She explained that at the beginning of every meeting, they assess previous changes to determine successful and unsuccessful changes. Then, every Thursday, a CAB (Change Advisory Board) meeting is held with IT Directors, where the meeting is recorded, and changes are either rejected or approved.

Then, I asked how many changes we have on a weekly basis, “She replied around 10-15 changes per week.”

She informed me that one of my team members, Ray, was known for putting changes into production without following the proper process. I promised her to follow up closely with Ray on this matter.

CHAPTER 3

THE CHALLENGES

"Until you dare to take on new challenges, you won't discover your full potential."

~ Bernard Kelvin Clive

It was an exciting day for me because I was about to attend my first management meeting at *CRN Design Canada*. When I logged on to the call, Richard introduced me to all the company's five IT directors. Also, there was a presentation prepared by Jim, the IT Help Desk manager. I heard Francisco telling Jim that he was receiving a lot of complains about wait time from the help desk to respond to phone calls. Then, Francisco asked Jim how long it was taking his team to respond to tickets. Unfortunately, Jim was not able to provide this information to Francisco.

Meanwhile, I asked Mary beside me while on mute, "Do we have SLAs (Service Level Agreements) in this company?"

"No! We don't! But we have SLOs (Service Level Objectives)," – Mary replied.

This means that we have a time limit to acknowledge a ticket, but we are not obliged to resolve tickets at a specific time. Clearly, Francisco was not happy about the Help Desk's performance. As a follow-up, Francisco requested another presentation from Jim in the next meetings with proper Key Performance Indicators (KPIs).

Measurement is the first step that leads to control and eventually to improvement.

Lessons Learned:
Make sure to measure your outputs to properly plan, comply, control, optimize, and innovate.

Diving into my work, the first thing I asked Ronald was to initiate a mini project of the installation of SCCM on all servers so we could get an accurate inventory list of our servers. SCCM is a Microsoft System Center Configuration Manager, which is a Windows product that enables the management, deployment, and security of devices and applications across an enterprise.

We commonly use SCCM for endpoint protection, patch management, and software distribution. On my side, I was aware that this project would take time because we had around 1400 servers, out of which around 700 were production servers.

Nevertheless, we absolutely needed to patch those servers and upgrade their outdated operating systems for security purposes. Moreover, our contracts manager, Jenny Dawson, was asking me for a list of servers to ensure they were all covered under an insurance warranty.

I started working on an improvement plan. In my fourth week, I submitted the plan to Richard. The improvement plan outlined the following items:

1. Establish a complete list of network devices and servers with their associated locations
2. Obtain a list of applications on each server
3. Classify applications based on their criticality (Gold, Silver, Bronze)
4. Establish KPIs for tickets and infrastructure monitoring metrics
5. Monitor my team's capacity (workload)
6. Collaborate and follow up with security & project team to ensure successful roll-out of initiatives.
7. Coach team members and provide guidance to lead them towards their career objectives
8. Create a culture where security and accountability are the responsibility of everyone.

Richard was happy with my improvement plan, but he requested an ETA (Estimated Time of Arrival or Delivery) for each of the initiatives. Therefore, I reported to have all the tasks completed in the next three months.

Lessons Learned:

Create value by properly prioritizing your tasks to continuously deliver. Always start with the shortest task first. In this way, things will always be moving.

As for big initiatives, divide them into smaller parts and continuously release those parts. This is how you start to become an agile thinker.

I rolled up my sleeves and started the real work. One of the initiatives in the improvement plan was to build a critical applications list. I wanted to start with the shortest task first to deliver value.

One of the discussions that I had with the team was related to this topic. How did the help desk team triage and prioritize their tickets if they did not have a proper critical systems list? This was causing frustration and affecting my team as well; if there was no list, that meant that the help desk team was treating all tickets with the same priority.

I verified the number of tickets in the ITSM system, and indeed, most of the tickets were opened as P4s. We needed to build an inventory list very soon. So, I started doing interviews with the IT specialists to build a proper list of all the applications that we support. I have included below a sample of how the list looked as we started documenting it.

We needed the following information: Application Category (Gold, Silver, Bronze), Application Name, Version, Availability Required, Product Owner Name, Application SME, Infrastructure SME, Targeted Users, DR Required.

Category	Business Application Name	Version	Availability Required	Product Owner Name	Application SME	Infrastructure SME	Target Users	DR Required
Gold	IndigoERP	7.4-7.6	24-Jul	Chris Jackson (CFO)	Josée Pierre	Ray Smith	CRN Design Employees	Yes
Gold	HRIS	2010-2013	24-Jul	Diana Spencer (HR VP)	Spencer Jones	Valerie Hopkins	CRN Design Employees	Yes

With the effort of most of the IT team and after a few months of hard work, we were able to build a full applications list.

"Finally, one good thing was completed!" I said to myself. As I was looking up, I saw Chris staring at me. He said, "I heard what you are doing with the team and organizing the work around. I just wanted to say that we are happy to have you with us." I smiled back and thanked him.

Even though things were progressing, I was surprised to receive a weird email from Richard. It sounded like a warning email, and I was on probation for three months. Richard wanted me to give him a list of servers in a week.

OMG! My stress level increased to 200%. I could hear my heart pounding. I started sweating and breathing heavily. I knew if I did not deliver, I was going to be fired. As I was reading the email, Ronald was running towards me, and he was yelling: "P1! We have a Priority 1 incident!"

According to Information Technology Infrastructure Library ITIL 4, an incident is an unplanned interruption to a service or reduction in the quality of a service.

My voice could not come out, but I heard myself asking, "What happened?"

"All applications in Montreal's data center are down!" Ronald replied.

"Darn it! Ok! Let's open a bridge, and please bring all SMEs to the call," I said to Ronald.

"SMEs?" Ronald said with a puzzled face.

"Subject Matter Experts – your key infra guys!" I exclaimed.

Ronald replied while putting his headset on, “Ok. Ok.”

I looked at my laptop’s clock – it was 11 a.m. eastern time. So, I asked, “Ok, who’s on the call? I see we have Ronald, Richard, Mary, Chris, Sandra, Raghu, and Valerie... more people are joining. Can someone identify the issue, please, and its impact?”

Ronald said, “We checked, and our virtual center had crashed. SAN is inaccessible.”

(SAN, an acronym for storage area network, is a computer network that provides access to consolidated, block-level data storage. SANs are primarily used to access data storage devices, such as disk arrays and tape libraries from servers so that the devices appear to the operating system as direct-attached storage.)

“We tried to reboot the hosts, but it is not working” - Paul, our SAN expert, commented.

I noticed there were around 20 people on the call: “Ok, Sandra, can you please take care of noting down what services are down? Also, please open a case with the vendor immediately.”

“Copy that,” - Sandra replied.

“Mary, please send communication to all of our employees informing them that we are having technical issues and we will keep sending an update every 20 minutes." – I said.

"I am on it," – Mary stated.

Sandra listed, "Those are the impacted Services: ERP system (Enterprise Resource Planning), HRIS (Human Resource Information System), Intranet, Email, Lync, FTP (File Transfer Protocol), VPN (Virtual Private Network), CRM (Customer Relationship Manager), Data Warehouse, Microsoft Project, Geomatics applications, Contract Management software and SharePoint."

"We can't send communication emails because email is not working" – Mary said.

My hand went on my head, and I said, "Yikes! Can we put a message on our phone system? Eventually, we will need to have a site where we display our systems' health, and people can view what systems are up or down on that site."

"Sorry to interrupt, but here is the case number with the vendor: 237346939," Sandra said.

Paul, while chewing his food, said: "Sorry, I'm eating... I have not eaten yet. So, servers are not coming back up. Three hours have passed, and no one has contacted us yet from the vendor."

I went offline for a couple of minutes, and then I replied, "Ok, I just escalated to the vendor's district manager. I don't understand. It is a P1 that we have opened with them. This is not urgent enough for them to contact us."

A few minutes later, a vendor, Level 3, pops up on our call.

Vendor support said, "Hi, this is Ishaan from the vendor support. How can I help you?"

"Paul, please explain to Ishaan our issue," I replied promptly.

Ishaan replied, "Paul, please email me the logs."

After an hour had passed... we were all silent on that call; then Ishaan broke the silence, and I got all excited, awaiting the resolution of the issue.

Ishaan said, "Just to let you know that my shift is now done, and now you will get another support person. Don't worry! We had logged all information in the ticket so the next person can continue working on this issue."

We all replied with the same disappointed voice, "Oh no! No!"

"Ishaan, we don't want to start from the beginning. Please assist us." – I commented.

Ishaan replied, "Madame, I have my colleague, Lakshmi; she will be your support moving forward."

A few minutes later... CIO Francisco pops in the meeting.

Francisco asks, "What's going on? Why this issue has not been resolved yet? When will the services be up?"

OMG! Francisco is here! That is all I needed. The CIO pressure. I thought to myself.

"Sir, we have an issue with our SAN, but we are fixing it. The vendor is involved."

It took Lakshmi around three hours to continue investigating on her side. We had to explain to her the issue all over again.

Then we heard Lakshmi saying, "Looking at the logs, let me do something... Ok. Hmmm *(a minute passed by). It should work now."*

Paul said, "I see the servers are coming back up. What did you do?"

Ronald excitedly said, "Everything is up. I was able to access a couple of applications, all good. I just checked with a couple of users, and all seem to work."

"Mary, please send an email that all is good and that services are accessible now, and do not forget to update our phone system." I requested politely.

Mary answered, "On it."

"Thank you," I replied.

Richard said, "This is the third time that this has happened. Guys, figure out what is the root cause of this issue."

"Francisco and Richard, we will prepare a major incident report and provide it to you in two days. We need some time because we must speak with the vendor first. Thank you, team! And thank you, Lakshmi. Have a good evening, everyone!" I said.

Francisco thanked us and logged off the call.

As I was walking in the hallway, I met Richard, who seemed unhappy. He said while shaking his head, "I do not understand why Francisco had to join the bridge. I was updating him continuously."

I replied with Ronald's famous response, "No comment." He told me that I did a good job managing this incident.

As I was looking at my watch, I was surprised to realize that it was already 8 pm. I knew I was going to arrive late and was not going to be able to see the kids, but I still had hope to see them before they went to sleep.

As I was riding the subway, I was thinking I must find the root cause of the data center issue. Richard said that it was the third time that this had happened. I closed my eyes for a second, but I was too tired and fell asleep on the subway.

Darn it! I missed my exit! Oh no! *(I sighed)*

It's Murphy's law: "Anything that can go wrong will go wrong." When you are speeding to get home, things don't work out, and you arrive late. So, I arrived home at 10 pm, and I was too tired to even talk with anyone, so I headed directly to bed.

The next day, my kids were having breakfast in the kitchen. So, my little son, Joey, started telling me about his fight with his friend at school.

"Mommy, my friend Jimmy threw a rotten banana on me during science class yesterday, and everyone started laughing at me."

"Ah…hum…yes," – I commented.

He intelligently said, "Mommy, repeat what I just told you… what was I saying?"

"I heard you. You had a fight with your friend... there was some sort of conflict," – I said.

He sadly replied, "What was that fight about?"

"You were fighting over something...an eraser?" I said while looking at him.

"Never mind...you weren't even listening to me" – Joey said with sadness.

Indeed, Joey was right. I was too occupied with the issue we had yesterday with the SAN, and I was determined to find the root cause. Also, what was worrying me was that if I was not able to find the root cause, would they fire me?

My husband, Eddie, approached me and whispered, "Every job you take, you try so hard to prove yourself. You put in so many hours, and you show your managers that you are responsible, so they give you more work. Why do you do that? Just do your work only and regular working hours."

I looked at him and said, "Honey, I am an IT operations manager. My job is to keep the green lights on. If I have one critical server down, the company loses millions of dollars because they can't deliver their projects on time. Imagine having an entire data center down. Never mind! You can't understand my work... *(speaking with disappointment)* It is very different from your accounting work."

CHAPTER 4
THE COMMITMENT

"You can never cross the ocean unless you have the courage to lose sight of the shore."

~ Christopher Columbus

Back in the office, I held my first meeting with the vendor virtually to discuss the data center issue. The vendor could not determine the root cause and advised us to upgrade the firmware of the SAN. Paul got all upset on the call and said, "This is the second time you advised us to upgrade the firmware, and we already did that."

I replied to the vendor fiercely, "This is not acceptable! This is the third time this has happened! Go back to the history of this incident, review all the logs you have, and come back with a definite root cause analysis. This incident is causing us to lose millions of dollars with major systems going down. We need this information in the next three days. Understood?" They said, "yes."

Surprisingly, Richard came out of his office with a tall old man wearing a suit. They started walking towards my desk.

I greeted Richard warmly, "Hi Richard!"

Richard said, "Hi Catherine, meet Francisco."

I stood up from my desk, feeling dizzy and shocked at the same time. I said, "Mr. Francisco, nice to finally meet you sir."

Francisco replied, "Likewise Catherine."

Richard asked while looking at me, "Would you mind joining us in the office?"

"Sure," I said

Entering Richard's office, what caught my attention was an entire wall made of glass overseeing downtown. The outside view was magnificent. We were on the 5th floor in downtown Montreal. I could see people walking on Sherbrooke Ouest. By the way, I rarely meet with Richard in his office... most of our meetings were in the conference room or out in the hallway with the team.

Francisco's deep voice interrupted my thoughts: "We have to resolve the data center issue."

I nodded in agreement.

Then, he continued with the conversation, "I was listening to your discussion with the vendor *(I smiled with a surprise look),* and I really like your professionalism. I am counting on you, Catherine. In the next two weeks, I need this resolved."

"Yes sir." I shook Francisco's hand and went back to my desk.

Humility is a great quality of leadership. A humble leader will get more respect from his staff instead of being feared or hated.

Lessons Learned:

No matter how high up you rise the leadership ladder, stay humble. Greet all employees equally.

As I was sitting on my desk, focusing on my plan, I heard Ronald mumbling, "You know...He did not even say hi to me." I looked up at Ronald and replied with sympathy, "Oh! You know CIOs, maybe he was worried about all his responsibilities. Don't take it personally Ronald."

Ronald replied with a sad voice, "no comment."

After a few hours, I saw Francisco leaving our office. He was probably flying back to his Toronto office.

I walked up to Richard and said, "The company's management team is upset because critical services are inaccessible, right? *(He nodded in agreement)* What if the vendor or the team couldn't find the root cause? Can we work on a parallel idea?"

Richard said, "I am listening, what's on your mind?"

"Replicate critical services to the backup data center." – I said.

"That's a big project and it will take a lot of time!" – Richard exclaimed.

"Let's start with the ERP system first. We have a smart DBA – Sean. Let's see if he can do it." I suggested anxiously.

Richard stopped everything he was working on, and instantly called our DBA, who was in our Ottawa office.

"Sean, how are you? We need your opinion on something. I have Catherine with me." Richard said with an exciting voice.

"Sure, what's up?" Sean replied.

Richard asked, "Can you replicate our ERP database to the Toronto data center? How much time will it take?"

"A week and a half with everything that I am doing right now. Also, I will need someone from the network team and someone from the applications team. What about our CRM? Do we replicate it as well?" Sean asked.

Richard said, "Let's do the ERP first, then we will think of the CRM next."

Creative thinking generates ideas and ideas generate change.

Lessons Learned:

Always think out of the box. Try to find alternative ways to resolve an issue.

In the biweekly management meeting, I sat in the conference room with Richard and Chris while Sean and Marc were on the phone with us. We all were direct reports of Richard. *I was not sure why Sean was not included in my team as he was operations DBA. I wondered quietly.*

Chris started the meeting by explaining that he had performed penetration tests, and he gave the status of his action items. He pointed out that there was no major risk in his findings. Then, Marc displayed his project portfolio and started presenting the health of his projects. He said he needed more staff from my team to support the Evergreening Project and to setup a new office. Then Richard went on to highlight the data center issue and emphasized that this issue needed to be fixed.

I went back to my desk, and the scrum meeting was already on. When I logged on, the team was all arguing about something, and Ronald was trying to calm them down. I greeted everyone, apologized for being late, and asked what the problem was.

Lessons Learned:

In the mid of a crisis or a problem, always stay calm and positive. How you react in this situation will be mirrored to your team members. Leaders and members of a team will all need to be calm to think properly and react wisely.

Ray replied, "Tickets keep on coming to us from the help desk with no details. They don't even do their first investigation... Darn it! This has been occurring for a very long time, and we can't continue working like this."

Then I said, "Is this issue with a particular person in the help desk team or is everyone not inputting information?" I received several replies saying everyone was in the helpdesk.

"Ok, let's establish an SOP, a standard operating procedure, to assist the help desk team during triaging." The team started complaining. Valerie said, "Why is this our problem now? They are not doing their job properly."

I replied with a smile *(I know they can hear the tone of my voice via the call; when I reply with a smile, it sends positive vibes to my team),* "Well, we are all here as one team. We are all working for one organization. We serve *CRN Design* employees and the community. Maybe they don't know what to investigate and what data to input. Let's help them, and in this way, we will reduce our tickets. It is a win-win situation."

Blaming or complaining about certain people or a situation do not resolve a problem. Instead, it consumes your energy and time, which you will absolutely need. Instead focus on collaborating with those people to create a solution and improve the situation.

Lessons Learned:

Avoid complaining in the workplace. Instead, contribute to creating a positive and healthy environment.

I went on to create the template for the SOP and placed it on SharePoint for all my team to contribute to evolving this document. After a couple of days, I followed up to find that no one had updated the file. So, to get the SOP filled out, I had to book a workshop with my team on the second day. During that workshop of two hours, most of the SOP was filled out.

After two sessions, we completed an SOP for our help desk with problems identified and proposed solutions to aid with their investigations. We indicated the type of data and requirements we needed for each issue. Ronald took the initiative of monitoring the progress and reported that tickets were reduced tremendously since we had given the SOP to the help desk. I was very content with this update.

Now that we are done with the SOP, I can finally focus on my data center issue *(I thought to myself)*. Suddenly, I heard Chris's loud voice coming from the conference room. *(Seemed like he was arguing with someone...there must be a serious issue, I said to myself.)*

Chris rushed out of the conference room, stood in front of my desk, and started swinging the chair while saying, "We need to patch all servers ASAP. The vendor discovered a security flaw, and it is a threat to the organization." Richard was approaching my desk as well. He said, "Catherine, initiate the patching and don't forget to open an emergency change request. We need all servers patched by the end of this week. Understood?"

All confused, I heard myself replying, "Yes sir."

My eyes were wide open with panic… There are thousands of servers that have to be patched all manually (I was thinking out loud). Darn it!

"Ronald, where are we with the SCCM installation?" I asked.

"10% complete," Ronald said.

"Oh my God!"

I went up to Richard and said, "Richard, I need Marc's team if I am to lead this security patching project. Do I have your consent?"

"Why?" Richard said.

"Because those servers have not been patched for years. If any of these servers does not come back up or have an issue, then we must rebuild the server from scratch." I clarified the issue to Richard.

Richard nodded and said, "OK, go for it."

So, I pulled both teams. I had around twenty people in total. I explained the plan.

Oh no! I need a list of servers... How can we patch without a proper list of servers? My God! I am thinking to myself and feeling helpless at the same time.

Suddenly, I remembered that Marc had mentioned to me that he had a tech-savvy guy who liked automation and was into innovation. I heard they compared this guy to Elon Musk, as they both were creative and came originally from South Africa. The name of the technical smart guy was Georges. So, I gave Georges a call as he was my only hope to get a servers list.

"Hi Georges, how are you? This is Catherine, the IT Infrastructure Operations Manager."

Georges *(speaking with a soft, respectful voice)*: "Hi Catherine, I know who you are. I heard a lot about you."

"Good things I hope?" I asked.

"Yes...Yes, all good." Georges replied.

"Georges, I need your help please. How can I get a list of all our servers? We need to patch all servers tonight and I don't have a list of servers." I said.

Georges replied to me with a question, "You asked the field engineer guys if they have one? What about Ronald?"

"Yes, I did. And no, we don't have a list *(the tone of my voice went low)*."

"Ok. Give me two hours and let me see what I can do." Georges said.

Three hours had passed by... And there was no reply from Georges. I tried contacting Georges, but I did not get any response.

Ronald kept looking at me. He heard my phone conversation with Georges.

"You know...He won't get you the list. Think of something else." Ronald said while looking at me.

(I frowned)

I asked the team to postpone the patching to the next day and updated Richard. I had a very tough night... I was having nightmares of not patching on time, our servers being hacked, and my name going on the news.

Early that morning, while having my coffee at the office to stay awake, Georges called me.

I jumped out of my chair, all excited, "Hi Georges, you got the list?"

"Yes, I worked on it all night," Georges replied.

"Awesome work! Thank you! Wow! You saved the day! I will for sure tell Marc and Richard all about your great work *(I heard Georges giggling while I was complimenting him).*"

So, we took the list and from the naming conventions, we were able to detect Dev, QA, and Prod servers *(At least they had proper naming conventions- I said to myself).*

On the same day, we sent notifications to *CRN Design* employees stating that we would process the patching of QA and Dev servers during working hours. As for production, we planned to patch after hours to avoid interruption of the business services during operational hours. We also opened an emergency change request as we needed to execute this change before the next CAB. The risk was high to wait until the next CAB.

Lessons Learned:

Always implement changes that impact your production services after business hours and make sure to properly communicate those changes to your stakeholders.

As for my patching plan, I directed the team to start patching production servers at 7 pm, after business hours, to avoid impact. I had prepared a plan to execute this patching change. My plan entailed the following:

I had divided the team into two teams. Every two hours, I was sending communication emails to the directors, updating them on our progress. Even though we got the servers list, we still had to patch all servers manually. After 10 pm, I dismissed one team so they could be ready to support the organization the next morning. This team would deal with any infrastructure issue that we could encounter after this change.

So, working back home at night, Eddie passed by my home office and said, "You haven't finished your work at the office? Why are you logged on?"

"Shh," I replied. "I am on a call. Wait… Let me go on mute. Please don't say anything. We must deal with this security issue. I have no choice. Please leave me alone. I don't have neither the time nor the energy to argue."

Eddie yelled, "THIS IS NOT A LIFE!"

For a couple of seconds, I remembered where was the work-life balance that I was promised in this company. A few minutes later, I reminded myself to stay positive, and things will for sure improve.

I stayed with the team on the conference call while they were patching all those servers until 3 am. Finally, we were done!

During the last half an hour, we became like drunk guys - joking and laughing for no reason.

I was extremely tired. I had a very bad headache, and I felt very sleepy. But I should not sleep now. Not yet. I still had to write the final email and update management.

I congratulated and thanked the team in an email and updated management. Now, I can go to sleep.

"Productivity is never an accident. It is always the result of a commitment to excellence, intelligent planning, and focused effort."
~Paul J. Meyer

Lessons Learned:

Work smart and hard. Working hard is rewarding. What is more rewarding is working smart! If you can automate tasks, optimize processes, create new ways of implementing a solution, that is smart work.

CHAPTER 5

THE DISAPPOINTMENT

" Don't raise your expectations too high. It's the surest way of being disappointed."

~Mary Louisa Molesworth

Eddie and I decided to finally buy a new house, so I took Friday off to focus on moving. Our family members were in the house helping us with the move when suddenly, I started getting several P1 notifications on my phone. Darn! It was the data center issue again *(speaking to myself with frustration)*. Quickly, I went up to Eddie and told him to cover for me while I had to work on the P1 issue. I sneaked to the bathroom, opened my laptop, and started a conference call.

This time, we had the ERP already replicated, so there was no impact there. Also, Mary had created a communication site with live updates on our systems' health. We were not relying much on emails anymore for communication. Nevertheless, we still updated the phone system with information about the outage to reduce the number of calls to our help desk.

Involving the vendor, I did not hesitate this time to directly escalate this issue to the vendor's VP. I provided him with a history of the data center's reoccurring issue and insisted on telling him that his team was taking too long to identify the source of the problem. He requested all case numbers that we have opened with them. Within an hour, he got a senior hardware engineer on the call with me.

The senior engineer said, "Hi Madame, I think we have a faulty switch at your data center, and it needs to be replaced."

"Are you sure?" I asked.

The engineer replied, "I was assigned to this problem a month ago and I have analyzed your logs along with the previous incidents. I highly recommend you replace the faulty switch."

I updated Richard and the team with this new news. And then, requested Ronald to open an emergency change request for the weekend to replace the faulty switch.

I went to Eddie and said, "I must go to the data center. We have a hardware issue which I need to take care of." Eddie looked at me, feeling very frustrated and said, "Go."

Ronald, Paul, and I spent the entire day with the vendor working in the data center, replacing the faulty switch. Once we were done, I requested Paul and Ronald to closely monitor the performance during the weekend. All that time, I was continuously updating Richard, who in turn was updating Francisco and the executive team on our progress.

Not knowing what to expect on Monday morning, I was rushing to arrive at work. Ronald was there already! He usually arrives at work at 7 am. He looked at me and with a smile he said, "All good! Don't worry. I have been monitoring the systems."

Feeling happy, I walked up to Richard's office and asked if we could proceed with replicating the rest of the critical services to our DR data center. He smiled while nodding in agreement.

One of the meetings I had that day was our regular biweekly management meeting with Francisco. Our happy CIO went on to recognize my team's efforts and congratulated us on working hard on stabilizing the systems. He told us to continue to monitor the systems closely.

As the directors were providing their updates, Richard announced that in the upcoming week, a new team lead of Infrastructure Architecture was going to join his team *(new news to me)*. Next, we moved on to listen to Jim's presentation on Help Desk KPIs. It seemed that Francisco was not impressed with Jim's final presentation because he did not ask a single question.

A few days later, we were surprised by two strangers waiting for Richard in his office. Ronald informed me those people were from central HR. Within a few minutes, Richard approached Ronald and said, "Ronald, disconnect Jim's account immediately."

Our eyes were wide open as we looked at each other. Then, we saw the HR staff going into Jim's office. As soon as Ronald disconnected the account, I reminded him to open a ticket for this request, and we asked Richard to approve this request in the ticket. A few minutes later, Jim, with a red face, rushed out of his office and left the building.

Later that day, we received an email from Francisco stating that Jim did not work at the organization anymore. The next day, I saw Mary moving her stuff to Jim's office. *(Ah! I kind of understand what was going on).* Ronald confirmed that Mary was taking Jim's position and that she was getting the IT Director title.

Wow… a lot of unexpected changes in the past few days.

I went back home feeling very disappointed. I had stabilized their systems, put in so many hours of my personal time, and yet there was no promotion or bonus for me.

Back home, Eddie felt my pain. "See, I told you, only do your hours. No one appreciates all your hard work. It is a game of politics," Eddie stated.

I replied with disappointment, "No comment."

In the office, I felt Richard started to change. He started to distance himself from us (his team). He barely had time for his direct reports after Mary got the promotion. Marc, Sean, and Chris had all complained to me that it had been a long time since any of us had a one-on-one meeting with Richard.

Even though the door of Mary's office was closed, I could hear some of her conversations. Mary was asking all the people around her for support and aid so she could be successful in her new role. When she attended our biweekly meetings with Francisco, the majority of the time of our meetings was spent on her updates.

Mary was loud and always asking questions and favors. She does ask smart questions sometimes, but she does not stop with questions. She was detail-oriented and had too much energy.

Be aware when going in a loop trying to figure out what your client, colleague, manager, or user wants. The simple way to get out of the loop is simply to have a meeting and ask direct questions.

Lessons Learned:

Do not get stuck trying to figure out what is wanted from you. Seek help and guidance.

One day, I said I wanted to check what Richard was helping Mary with, so I went into Mary's office. I knocked on the office door and said, "Richard, I need your advice on an issue."

They seemed very concentrated on a problem or certain topic. Both were looking at Mary's screen. "Do you guys want me to help you with anything?" I asked.

Richard replied, "We have been trying to figure out for the past four days if Francisco wanted only lagging metrics or leading metrics as well."

"Why don't you ask him?" I asked.

Richard replied, "We don't want to bother him."

With a smile, I said, "Trust me, he will be happy if you ask him what he wants."

"Maybe you are right," Richard said.

They called him while I was in the office and Francisco replied that he wanted both metrics. Also, he gave them more information exactly about his requirements.

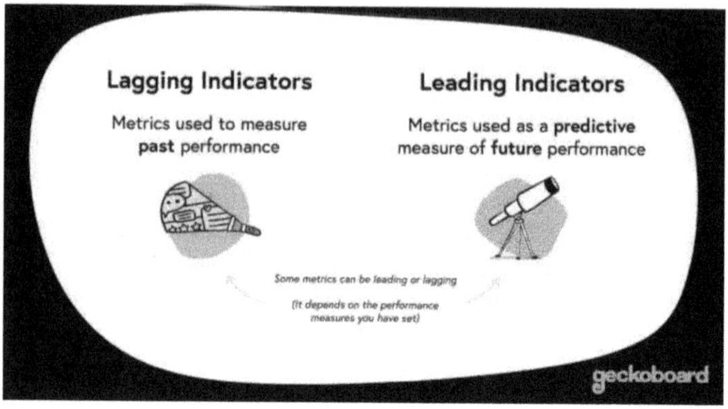

Walking back to my office, I noticed a very tall gentleman, dressed in a grey suit, sitting beside my desk. It was André Brault, the new infrastructure architecture team lead. He wanted a few minutes with me in the conference room to introduce himself and tell me about his plans.

André seemed very professional, with many years of experience in IT Infrastructure. He told me that Sean will be moving to his team in the upcoming few days, and he will be hiring two more architects. *Ah! Now I understood why Sean never reported to me. Richard had plans for Sean.*

Back in my own cubicle, I started working on the final incident report of the data center issue. After a few months, the vendor confirmed that the root cause of the data center failure was a hardware defect. I presented the incident report to the management team, and we were happy that this major problem was resolved once and for all. Also, I had lessons learned with my team to see what we could learn from this incident and make improvements for future incidents.

As I was chatting with Ronald, I told him, "I can't believe it is almost a year now working with you and the team. Time flies while having fun!"

Ronald replied with a smile, "Indeed, I like working with you - lady boss!"

"We accomplished a lot of things. I am so proud of Sandra. She won "employee of the month" because of delivering good quality projects. Also, Valerie is paying more attention to her work. Her productivity is shown in the quantity of deliverables she is producing. She stopped going on social media during working hours. I am so proud of her as well."

Ronald replied, "I agree! Great improvements... But not for Raghu though."

"I will give Raghu a few more chances. I know he does not attend all our meetings, but he does his work, right?" I asked.

Ronald replied, "That is because he only takes certain types of tickets and no projects. His excuse is that he does not know new network technologies. But why can't he learn, for God's sake!"

I replied, "No comment. Let's see how it will be in the annual performance evaluation. I will be flying with Richard across Canada to meet the team face-to-face for the first time."

It was my first yearly performance evaluation. I was looking forward to meeting the team! I thought to myself.

Recognizing employees who deliver good and hard work is very important. Employees will give back to the company when they know their work is well appreciated.

Lessons Learned:
Always recognize and appreciate your team members who work hard and contribute to the success of the team and the company.

In Calgary, I met Sandra, Ray, and Jonathan. After a couple of hours, Ron and Andy joined us as they drove from Red Deer. We ate Indian food during lunch and had so much fun talking about our personal lives. Sandra told me that she got a boyfriend now and bought an apartment. I was so happy for her. Also, she thanked me for believing in her and her capabilities.

I enjoyed spending time with this team. I found that they were all nice, respectful, and cheerful. We provided our feedback and remarked on Sandra's great improvement. We recognized her dedication to delivering all her tasks on time and with quality.

As for Ray, he had been following the change management process. He stopped performing changes without an authorized change request.

Once we finished the evaluations, the team decided they wanted to have Chinese food for dinner. This is when I started to get severe headaches, and I felt like vomiting. I asked to be excused and went back to my hotel. In my hotel room, I was sweating, shivering, and feeling very cold. I was crying from the pain that night. Then, I crawled to bed and slept. The reason I got sick, I think, was that I had a very long, intense day that started at 3 am, and I was not used to eating Indian and Chinese food on the same day. Thank God, the second day, I woke up feeling better.

After Calgary, we flew to Vancouver, where we met Angelo, Adam, and Azadeh. It was a great day in Vancouver, British Columbia. Even though it was my first time in Vancouver, I could not see much as we only did the evaluations at the *CRN Design* office and flew back to Toronto to meet the rest of the team.

In Toronto, I met with Anand, Mohamed, Raghu, and Steven. My one-to-one with Raghu was memorable. While I was with Richard doing Raghu's performance review, he ignored me completely. All his conversations and responses to my questions during the performance dialogue were directed at Richard. He only looked at Richard as if Richard was the only one in the office. I was blown away by this unprofessional behaviour.

After we completed the performance dialogue, Richard mentioned to me how disrespectful Raghu was. It was documented in his review that he did not try to learn new technologies and avoided taking on tickets and initiatives in areas that required his time to investigate.

Even though I was so happy to do the tour and meet my team during their performance evaluations, I was looking forward to coming back home to see Eddie and the kids. I missed them so much.

CHAPTER 6

THE PRICE OF SUCCESS

"The price of success is hard work, dedication to the job at hand, and the determination that whether we win or lose, we have applied the best of ourselves to the task at hand."

-Vince Lombardi

It was winter again in Montreal! Looking outside from my home window, I was listening to the morning news. They were announcing a freezing rain warning. Freezing rain occurs when the layer of freezing air is so thin that the raindrops do not have enough time to freeze before reaching the ground. Instead, the water freezes in contact with the surface, creating a coating of ice on whatever the raindrops come into contact with.

I felt so unlucky that I had to go to work downtown in this bad weather. It was not just freezing rain but blowing snow as well. The temperature was negative 20 Degrees Celsius (-20°C). I had put on my winter shoes, toque, gloves, and shawl in preparation to leave for the office.

I wished I could work from home, especially in such severe weather conditions. Unfortunately, my management team did not approve work from home unless there was a medical reason.

On my way out of the home, Eddie reminded me to ask Richard for a vacation. He said we could go to New York City, which is a five-hour drive from Montreal. So, first thing when I arrived at work, I headed to Richard's office to request my vacation.

"Good morning, Richard."

Richard smiled back and said, "Good morning, Catherine."

"Can I take a vacation for a couple of weeks to go to the USA with my family? You know, I have not taken a vacation since I have started working here," I asked nicely.

Richard replied, "Can you have your phone and laptop with you during your vacation, just in case we needed you?"

"Sure," I replied.

We took off to New York City and visited Time Square and the museums. It seemed like ages that we had not gone on a vacation. Eddie, the kids, and I really enjoyed the quality time together. While I was on vacation, I did get a couple of urgent notifications, but Ronald was kind enough to cover for me.

I bonded with my kids on that vacation. They were telling me about their friends, their plans for

---

Continuous work with no vacation time can make people feel sick, blocked, and have problems concentrating. Surveys show that people who took vacation time regularly felt more energized and ready to tackle the tasks at hand.

Lessons Learned:

Take your vacations throughout the year. It will help you feel healthier and ready to tackle your work challenges.

---

the summer, and their school challenges. I had an amazing time with Eddie as well.

Vacation passed by very fast. We felt like we needed a vacation after the vacation. So, back in the office, I had a big smile on my face. I was in "vacation mode." I was thankful to my great team, boss, and colleagues. I knew I was really blessed to belong to this great organization. Above all, I never got bored. There were always new things coming my way. For example, one of the projects that got prioritized by management was the SOX compliance project.

Chris and Richard approached me and said that they needed me to participate in the SOX compliance project. They announced that this project was a priority project over all other projects.

All U.S. public companies are required to comply with the Sarbanes-Oxley Act (SOX), which was created to increase the accuracy and transparency of corporate disclosures in financial statements and to protect investors from fraud accounting practices through effective risk management. To achieve SOX compliance, a company must meet all the requirements outlined in its SOX report.

They had assigned Raul Rodriguez from *CRN Design USA* as the IT project manager on this project. As I reviewed all the requirements, we were missing some processes. So, I started accumulating existing processes and documenting processes that did not exist. Because we were handling operational work during working hours, sometimes I had to work on weekends to document those missing processes, including the backup process, disaster recovery process, and the access management process. This project took around four months. After we had established all our processes, we got audited by an external consulting company.

Something weird happened to me during this project. At some point during the project, Raul escalated to Richard that I needed more resources to complete my upcoming work on time. Even though I assured Raul that I could meet the deadline, he insisted on having a virtual meeting with Richard.

Richard asked me, "Do you need assistance in completing your work?"

"No, I will complete it this week," I replied anxiously.

Raul interrupted me and said, "Excuse me Richard. We have analyzed the work pending for Catherine, and it is two resources full time for three weeks to complete the work. Catherine can not complete all this work by herself! I repeat she can not. Sorry Catherine, but this is too much work for you, and you need help." *I was surprised by the comment.*

Richard then asked, "Catherine, what do you need so we can complete this project?"

"I need three resources full-time for the next two weeks," I replied very seriously.

"Ok. Let me see what I can do." Richard said.

I felt they would not let me off the call until I told them that.

On the second day, I headed to Richard's office and told him that I had completed the work required for SOX. I explained that Raul could not believe me last week when I told him that I needed a week to finish the work.

All I can say is that after that SOX project, all the IT PMO members treated me differently. I earned myself a reputation that I complete things half-time and that I can exceed expectations.

A few days after we finished the SOX project, we received an email from Francisco informing us that *CRN Design Canada* had passed the SOX audit with the highest compliance rate compared to other *CRN Design* offices in other countries.

I was so happy when I received a special email from Francisco recognizing my great performance.

On the subway, while I was heading back home, I was consuming and digesting the information that I was reading in *The Phoenix Project*. That was a great IT novel by Gene Kim, Georges Spafford, and Kevin Behr. The main character of the story was the VP of Operations, who was struggling with similar IT issues like me. It was a very interesting novel that I recommended to my team to read.

"All Leaders are readers"
~Jim Rohn

Lessons Learned:
Read one book a month.

In every scrum, I reminded my team that security and quality were everyone's responsibility. Also, I knew that not all my team members had knowledge about Cloud. Therefore, I requested from Richard that my team members get the proper training on cloud, and he accepted.

One of the objectives I wanted to introduce in my company was to align IT with the business. *Why not have IT ambassadors at the business level? I was thinking to myself.*

The next day, I pitched the idea to Richard. I told him we need Business Relationship Managers (BRM) because we need to be closer to the business and ensure we are tackling the issues and future projects they have for us. In his turn, Richard proposed this idea in the executive management meeting, and Francisco liked it. Right away, Francisco assigned his IT Directors an additional role, which was the Business Relationship Manager role. Finally, we started to hear from the business on things that we can improve.

For example, the Geomatics department had complained regarding slowness in their applications. And they requested us to find a solution. We got the applications team involved, as well as the DBAs. We added more resources (memory and disk) from the infrastructure side, and the DBAs also optimized some of the SQL statements to improve performance and normalize the database. We started monitoring those applications closely as we better understood their criticality. The Geomatics engineers were very happy with the performance improvement.

Their director even sent a "Thank you" note to Francisco.

It is very important to ensure business agility. Having Business Relationship Managers bridged the gap between our business and IT. We were able to reduce technical issues across the organization and delivered alternative solutions via projects for things we could not fix. Our industrial engineers were able to deliver their projects faster and with quality due to our rapid service delivery and our good relationship.

Now, two years have passed at this amazing company. I was very happy that my voice and recommendations to management were all being

The unexpected had happened.

heard and I was being appreciated. Also, I was blessed to have a wonderful team who we all worked together and exceeded expectations on our deliverables. All was going well until something unexpected happened.

There were circulating rumors about outsourcing the IT team. Mary was talking about it; she said she heard it from the global team. Also, I heard it from other people as well, but I kept dismissing this rumor. *No way this company will outsource us, I said to myself.*

One day, I saw Francisco dropping by without any notice. He met with Richard privately. A few hours later, I was informed that some of my team members received an email about outsourcing the IT department to an external consulting company. I asked to be forwarded the email. My brain could not make any sense of what I was reading.

CHAPTER 7

THE SURPRISE

"Ships don't sink because of the water around them; ships sink because of the water that gets in them. Don't let what's happening around you get inside you and weigh you down."

~Unknown

Confidential Employee Memo

From: Francisco Sanchez
January 15, 2016
CRN Design Canada
Full-Time IT Employees

CRN Design Canada continues to transform its business and realign resources accordingly. We have worked hard to adapt to changes brought on by the challenges of our changing business model and current economic environment at the same time to serve our customers and community.

Although our efforts have been successful by several measures, additional adjustments are needed to properly align our costs with operating revenues. Therefore, to reduce payroll expenses, we are announcing a voluntary severance program which will be offered to our IT full-time employees.

The offer is as follows: Employees who accept this offer and who sign the release agreement will receive (10) days of severance pay at their base rate, for each year of service completed, with a minimum of 10 days and a maximum severance amount of 26 weeks of pay.

Employees with 20 years or more of service will receive 56 weeks of pay. Service shall be determined based on the number of FULL years completed with the company, with the exception being that if the termination date falls 60 days or less before a service anniversary, then this last year of service shall be counted as a full year.

If you have an interest in this offer, please sign the attached form, and return it by Monday, January 25, 2016.

Please understand that even though you express interest in this offer by submitting the attached form, the company will determine who will be selected based on a variety of business factors. After the company has considered all the employees who have expressed interest in the offer, only those who are selected by the company will receive the actual voluntary severance agreement for further consideration.

If you are selected to receive the voluntary severance offer, your employment will end on July 31, and you will have 45 days to consider the offer from the date you receive the agreement. If you accept the offer, you have seven days after the 45-day period to revoke your acceptance.

This is a voluntary offer, and your decision should be based on your individual personal assessment and circumstances.

Francisco Sanchez

CIO CRN Design Canada

This is the email that Francisco sent to some of our IT members. I did not get this email; not sure what that meant, but I wanted to consult with Richard to see what the plan of the executive team was.

I headed to Richard's office. Richard's face was white as a ghost. I asked him if he had a few minutes for me. He said yes. So, I sat in his office and closed the door.

"Richard, what's going on?"

"They are outsourcing IT," Richard said.

With frustration, I asked, "All IT?"

"Well, the new company will get some of our SMEs, who you and I must identify. *A few seconds of silence passed by.* Our expectation is that most of the people will wait for the next six months to get their severance package. Otherwise, they can leave at any time with no compensation. On August 1st, *TNR Global IT,* a global IT consulting company, will take over all our work." Richard explained.

"What about you, Richard? What will happen to you?"

"In the next few days, they will announce that I will join the global team as the Global Director of Infrastructure Canada, and I will be working from now until August on ensuring there is proper knowledge transfer of knowledge between our team and the new vendor," Richard replied.

"Are we keeping the SMEs?" I asked.

"Very few. Handful of people. Probably one person for each area."

"Ouf! What about if SMEs decide to leave now?" I asked.

"We will be giving out retention bonuses to keep the guys we want to keep."

"Ok. What about me? I did not receive the letter from Francisco. What does that mean?" I asked sadly.

Richard answered with a smile, "Don't worry, you are safe."

What did he mean by safe? I didn't understand.

Meanwhile, the silence was interrupted by a shy knock on the door. It was Mary.

Mary said, "You guys... You heard what happened? They are outsourcing us."

I replied with an upsetting voice, "Yes, we heard."

Then Mary said, "By the way, I have lived this before in my previous life. They outsourced us and

I ended up collaborating with the new company and transferring the knowledge. They then offered me a job at the new IT Consulting company. We should show our collaboration and work with the outsourcing company. They might transfer us to the new company."

What did I just hear? I thought to myself. She wants us to collaborate.

I am trying to digest the information I just heard from Mary. She was speaking with enthusiasm, but I was feeling very sad and disgusted. They are taking our jobs away, and she wanted us to collaborate.

Many of my team members started chatting with me on Teams. My heart was chattering away with all these messages. I felt as if I was on a train track and a train was coming to wreck me.

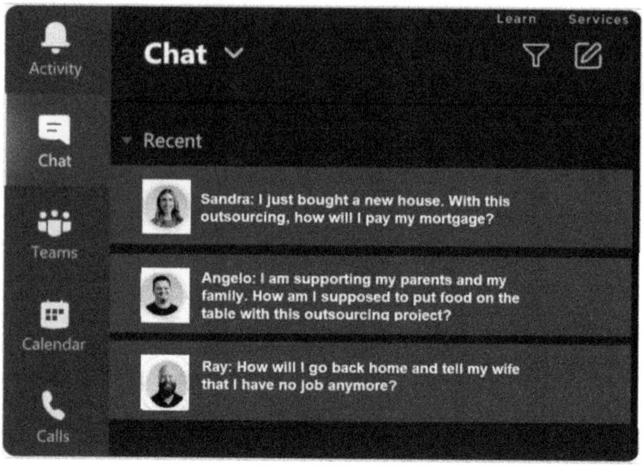

The second day, Richard called me to his office and told me that Marc had accepted an internal transfer as a project manager for the Geomatics department. I was blown away.

I asked Richard, "Why did Marc do this? He does not care about his team?"

Richard replied, "I don't know, but I need you to take over his team, ok?"

I replied, "Sure."

I booked a meeting with Marc's team and informed them that they will report to me moving forward. I had received several questions from his team about the outsourcing project, but I had no answers for them.

I reviewed all infrastructure projects and booked meetings with Marc's team to get updates on the status of the projects. I needed all the information, so I could continue managing the projects.

So now, I was handling my infrastructure operations team and the projects team. I had a network P1 issue. I asked my network engineers to investigate. Raghu, as usual, had so many reasons to avoid this investigation. This is when I decided to build a case to let Raghu go and present it to HR. I documented all historical events when Raghu was not collaborative and misbehaved and attached them to his file. Also, I made sure to include his performance evaluations and feedback. For two weeks, I was awaiting Francisco's approval to let go of Raghu. When I did not get any response, I decided to contact Francisco.

Francisco answered my call: "Hi Catherine. How are you?"

"Good sir. I don't want to take much of your time, but I wanted to know what happened to Raghu's file. Any progress?" I asked.

Francisco asked, "Are you sure of your decision?"

"Yes sir. I gave Raghu multiple chances, and I did not see any improvement. Also, I need to hire his replacement." – I replied.

Francisco then said, "Ok, we will proceed with this. I will send my approval right away, but you can't hire his replacement because of the outsourcing project. There is a hiring freeze."

I replied with a disappointed voice, "How will I continue to work and keep the company functioning for the next six months with no resources?"

Francisco said, "Hire consultants."

"Ok sir. Can I ask you, if it is not too much, what will happen to me?" I asked.

Francisco replied, "You are a star, Catherine! You are top-notch professionally. You should not worry!"

"Am I staying?" I asked in a hesitating voice.

"Yes," Francisco replied with an affirmative voice.

I sighed! I felt so relieved!

"Thank you, sir. Thank you very much!" - I exclaimed.

Francisco laughed and said, "Ok. Bye Catherine."

As I was hanging up with Francisco, I saw a message from Richard on Teams to go to his office. So, I knocked on Richard's office door.

Richard said, "Catherine, where are you? I have been waiting for you to come for the past half an hour."

"Sorry Richard. I was with Francisco."

Richard replied, "When your boss calls you, you come immediately. Understood?"

Wow! It was the first time I got this negative attitude from Richard.

"But… but, I was with Francisco, your boss." - I uttered.

Richard replied, "Who is your boss?"

"You," I replied.

Then, I asked Richard, "What can I do for you?"

Richard said, "Mary has just resigned."

"Come again?" I requested Richard to elaborate.

Richard said, "Mary is leaving in two weeks. She found another job and she is leaving."

"Oh my God! What about the collaboration? And working together with the new IT consulting company so they can hire us. What happened to all that?"

Richard replied, "No comment."

Then he said, "Catherine, can you take her place?"

"I am doing Marc's work and my work. You want me to take over the help desk team as well?" I replied with an enormous rage.

Richard replied, "Listen, they are outsourcing, and it is not a good time to say no."

"Understood. Ok I will take it."

I understood the hidden message: if I don't take the work, they will let me go.

"Good. I will ask Mary to transfer her knowledge to you. You will be presenting weekly stats to management in her place and leading the help desk team."

I nodded, "Ok."

For the next two weeks, I spent my time with Mary in training. She showed me how to set up the help desk phone system and the weekly KPIs. Not sure why Mary had decided to leave because I heard from Richard that they had a great position for her in the global team.

Anyhow, I took her office when she left. Most of the people on that floor were reporting now to me. Overall, now, I had a total of around fifty-five employees. To manage all of this team, I was working after hours and on weekends.

When Mary left, and for the next twenty days, almost every other day, one member of her team knocked on my door to give me his resignation letter. I contacted a consulting company and was hiring consultants like crazy. In the end, I was left with three employees of the original help desk team, and the rest of the team were all new people.

Yet, I managed to keep the green lights on. My KPIs were still looking good. Few escalations. Instead of putting the new people to be trained one-on-one with existing employees, we created videos because we were tired of repeating the same materials over and over again to the new employees.

In my original team, every month, I had one person leave. We had engineers onsite with us from the new consulting company receiving the transfer of knowledge. I was supervising and ensuring there was proper ongoing communication between the new IT consulting engineers and our team.

In one of my discussions with Richard in his office, he told me that the global team had another plan for me. He said they wanted me as the Service Delivery Manager in the new IT consulting company.

I asked Richard, "Why me? Who will I be dealing with on the *CRN Design* side if I accept to go to the new company? I apologize for all these questions. I am just trying to understand the thought process behind this decision."

Richard answered, "Me. You will be dealing with me."

"Ah ok! And how many people will report to you on the *CRN Design* side?" I asked.

"Three: Paul, Ronald and Sean," Richard answered.

I waited for five seconds and then I said, "Hmm... There are still three months before the outsourcing cutover date. Maybe I should find another job. I don't want to go to the new company! What about if I said no?"

"I highly recommend you don't say no to the global team." – Richard replied.

Then I asked, "Richard, why are you staying? Why are you not seeking opportunities elsewhere?"

Richard replied, "This outsourcing project is good on my CV."

I agree with Richard about the usefulness of adding this experience to my CV as well.

As I was working on an incident report, Francisco contacted me for some reports. I took this opportunity to ask him about my status in the company.

"Francisco, you know what good work I have done at this company so far. Right?"

"Yes." – Francisco replied.

"How does my future look like within your team? Can I become an IT Director for Canada? The entire department is functioning because of me today, you know that. I can lead the procurement team and data team if you want. What do you say?"

Francisco replied, "Let me think about it and I will get back to you next week."

The same week, I was contacted by the director of the new IT consulting company, Justin

Lake. He wanted an interview with me for the IT Service Delivery Manager, and I accepted.

Justin Lake was a very nice gentleman. He told me that his organization was a global organization but had no offices in Quebec. *CRN Design* was their first client in Quebec. He made me a decent offer, but I had to reject it.

I was thinking to myself: If, for whatever reason, I did not get along with Richard or his successor in the future, I would not have a job because they only have one client in Quebec, which is *CRN Design.* So they can not assign me to any other client. It did not make sense to me to accept this position.

Continuing to struggle with all these challenges, my biggest shock was when Ronald contacted me. He told me he was leaving to work in an IT company beside his house. Ronald was one of the retained employees with over 20 years of experience at *CRN Design.* Also, I loved working with Ronald. This news made me very sad and disappointed.

CHAPTER 8
THE MISERY

"Be Brave. Take risks. Nothing can substitute experience."

~Paulo Coelho

Shuffling people to keep the lights on was extremely challenging and time-consuming. Most of my daily tasks were onboarding and offboarding the employees, managing the IT operational tasks, and leading some ongoing projects.

A couple of people who were on my original team stayed until the end. Even Sean and Paul refused to stay, even though they were offered a retention bonus. Paul told me on his last day, "I don't want to stay in a company that treats its employees in this way. We are just numbers to them!"

One day, while I was onboarding a consultant, I got a phone call from Ray.

"Ray! How are you?" I asked.

Ray said, "Oh! You know... Surviving."

"Ray, you sound awful. Is everything ok?" I asked.

Ray answered, "Nothing related to work... I am getting divorced."

"Oh my God! Ray! I am so sorry to hear this news. Anything I can do to help?"

Ray replied, "No... but this is not why I called you. I called you to tell you I have transferred the knowledge to the two new engineers, and I am just looking after tickets now."

"Ok. Ray, you are staying with us until the end?"

"I am doing interviews, but I have not received any job offer yet." – Ray replied.

Then, I said, "Ok. How about I book you for an interview practice tomorrow? And send me your CV please so I can check it out and advise you on improvements."

Ray replied, "Ok. Will do. Thank you."

As I hung up the call with Ray, I noticed there were two HR people waiting for me outside the office. I asked them what I could do to help them. They had a list of employees they needed to execute termination immediately.

With a very pale face, I said, "Excuse me... Please repeat."

HR said slowly, "We need you to call, one at a time, each person listed here into the conference room, and we have a document that you must read to each one in our presence. Then, we will explain their severance package to them."

I felt like I was wrecked by a train hearing this news.

There were around twenty-five names on that list! With sadness, I started to call people one by one inside the room. While I was reading the text, I could hear my heart beating fast, and I was sweating.

I couldn't hear the people well as I was reading their termination letters. Some started crying, and others got extremely angry. I had a couple of people were smiling and laughing, which was extremely weird. We were in a very awkward situation.

HR staff were accompanying the people to grab their items and guiding them outside the company.

At the end of that day, there were only six of us on that floor besides the consultants.

It was the most miserable day of my life. I kept rewinding the memories and felt very sad.

That weekend, I had a car accident. I was picking up my daughter Annie from her friend's house. Driving back home, I crashed into another car. I was so occupied thinking about the outsourcing project that I did not pay attention when the car in front of me stopped. Thank God no one got injured, but it was a memorable moment.

CHAPTER 9
THE REBIRTH

"A pessimist sees the difficulty in every opportunity; an optimist sees the opportunity in every difficulty."

~Winston Churchill

Three weeks were left before the outsourcing project was launched. At this point, half of my team had gone to work for other organizations. And I had two people who went on sick leave. Now, most of my staff were consultants on contracts ending on July 31st.

Eddie advised me that if I wanted to keep my job, I must get closer to the global team. So, I asked Francisco if I could join the global team office in downtown Montreal to follow up on the outsourcing project, and Francisco accepted.

Also, in the same call, Francisco made a great announcement for me. He congratulated me on my great work and offered me the IT Director position. I became responsible for CRN Design Canada's IT Contracts Management Team, IT Assets Management Team, and IT Procurement Team. Finally, I felt my hard work was fruitful.

The next day, I headed to the office where the global team was working. I was surprised to see all the people working in an open space sitting in cubicles, and only three people had closed offices. One of those people who were in those glass offices was Richard. I waved to him, and he came and greeted me.

Richard congratulated me on my promotion and told me that the global team was not happy with Francisco giving me that promotion. He said they wanted me to go to the outsourcing company. I felt Richard was preparing me to expect some rejection from the global team.

Nevertheless, Richard went on to introduce me one by one to all the people in that office. There were around 35 people working in that office, including Justin Lake. Most of the global team members came from the USA just to execute this project. They told me they go back to see their families every other weekend.

I noticed that the global *CRN Design* team was like family more than colleagues. They were joking with each other all the time, and they went out to lunch together every day.

I noticed most of the global team were men. There were only two women on that floor: Sophie, the communication manager and me. I was not able to fit in – it was a weird atmosphere - yet I kept on trying.

One day, I entered the office and greeted the global VP, Sam McDonald. He replied in a weird voice and with a smile, "Hi lady in red." My eyebrows went out of my face... *What did that mean? Is that a flirt? That comment was not professional.*

Day after day, I was going to the office. I was alternating between this office and the other one to keep track of the other employees.

Richard used to come to my desk and tell me how miserable he felt in his new role. He also told me that one of my previous team members, Steven, had died shortly after he was let go from the organization. Apparently, he had cancer and did not tell anyone. (*Did he get sick because of the outsourcing project... I wondered)*

A week later, Richard said that his mom had a surgery, and he might take some time off to take care of her. He requested two weeks off from management as an urgent request.

"Oh my God! We will launch this project without Richard." I said to myself.

Before he left, Richard told the global team that I was the reference point for IT in Canada and that I could attend the global meetings on his behalf.

So, in the first global meeting after Richard's absence, I was not invited. The second meeting I was also not invited. I felt unwelcomed...

I was wondering, it was my chance to prove myself and why they were not calling me to attend their meetings. They had all global IT directors, but no IT representation from Canada.

On the other hand, I was in continuous communication with Francisco. He seemed super happy. Apparently, he was not getting any update on this project from the global team before.

So, on a deeper discussion with the transformation manager, I asked, "How will we be receiving tickets in the future?"

He replied, "There is a new instance of the ITSM system."

Then, I asked, "What about the old tickets?"

He replied, "We did not think of that *(1 week before Go Live and they did not think of that).*"

Then, I asked about the backup systems of all the servers. They did not have an answer for that as well. I felt that they were not in control.

On a Go-No-Go call, Sam, the global VP, asked if we were ready to launch. All the team answered that they were ready. When he asked if there were any risks, I interrupted and said, "YES."

He exclaimed, "Shut up Catherine!"

I was blown away… He tried to ask me later about what risk I wanted to state, but I replied that it was not important.

I was extremely upset by how and what Sam had responded to me in front of everyone. Anyhow, I wanted to warn them about some issues I have detected in the ITSM system.

On August 1st, the launch date, NOTHING WAS WORKING.

Tickets were not being opened. No team from the outsourcing company was receiving any ticket. They were working day and night to identify the issue. It took them two months to resolve the ticketing system issue. They had a backlog of tickets from 2 months in addition to the old tickets they had before.

Many industrial engineers started quitting their jobs because they were not getting their laptops delivered on time with the proper software installed. So, they could not deliver their work, and it showed that they were not working. Also, if they opened any IT request, no one was getting back to them.

So, one day, I was in the same meeting with Sam, the global VP. I said, "Did you read how many comments were posted on the company's website complaining about the new IT service management?"

With a disgusted smile, Sam replied, "It does not matter. We saved 40 million dollars by doing this outsourcing project."

Since that day, I started having severe headaches as if there were lightning in my head. I could not get rid of the pain.

All engineering departments were escalating and complaining about the outsourcer's poor service delivery. We had hundreds of engineers quitting every week, but we saved 40 million dollars, according to Sam.

So, one day, unexpectedly, Richard came up to me and said, "I just resigned."

"WHAT???" I yelled.

With a puzzled and surprised face, I replied, "Why?"

Richard said, "I am not happy with this work anymore. I like to help people, and I feel no one is listening here. They have an agenda in which they are following. Also, I like to do technical management. There is nothing technical in the work I do now."

Oh my God! This is becoming very intense.

Richard resigned on Friday, giving them two weeks' notice. The following Monday, while Richard was still on the job, one of our IT staff notified us that they saw an IT service request to create a new account username for his replacement.

What does that mean? They had his replacement before he resigned, or they were planning on letting him go beforehand, or the minute he resigned, they called a friend.

I WAS SHOCKED! I WAS LOSING ALL MY COLLEAGUES.

I decided to stay since I recently got promoted, and it would not look good on my CV if I left after a few months of getting promoted. I continued to work hard in collaboration with the global team. I was helping the global team in the next few months while managing my Canadian IT team as well. The global team very much appreciated my collaboration, and they went on to request Francisco to transfer me to their team.

Unfortunately, that was not my plan.

I was very satisfied working with Francisco and the Canadian IT team.

Francisco was kind enough to call me and ask my opinion about this proposition. He said," Catherine, the global team is asking that I transfer you to their team. Do you want to move to their team?"

"Francisco, I don't want to work different shifts to accommodate global countries. I really have enough work at *CRN Design Canada*. I like working with you and the other IT Directors. I don't want to move. Please." – I replied.

The next day, I was surprised with a meeting request from the global VP at 11 am inviting all IT Directors of *CRN Design Canada*, but NOT Francisco. Immediately, I sent an email to Francisco asking where he was and asked him why he was not invited to that meeting. I received no reply.

In that urgent management meeting, Sam announced that Francisco was let go, and they were seeking his replacement.

My God! What was happening? Francisco is fired! No!

Suddenly, I received a call from Francisco. He said, "Catherine, I am ok. Don't worry! They gave me a good severance package. One of the reasons that I was let go was that I did not accept to move you to their global team."

I could not control my tears. I replied, "No Francisco. This is not happening."

Francisco replied, "Don't worry! You are top-notch professionally and anywhere you go, you will excel. You are a great leader, and you must stay strong."

I replied with a very sad voice, "Thank you Francisco. I am so happy to have had the chance to work with you. I hope one day we will work together again! Goodbye for now."

My brain is not making sense of all this.

From that day onwards, I hated going to work. I could not control my tears and anger.

Two weeks later, Sam approached me and said, "Hi Catherine, I would like you to meet the new

CIO of Canada – Susan Smith. Please can you introduce her to the team and help her navigate the office? It is her first day today." I nodded as I said yes.

I welcomed the new CIO and introduced her to our IT members in that office. Then I went to call Richard in the hallway.

Phone ringing...

Richard answered, "Hello?"

"Hi Richard, It's Catherine. Can you please find me a job at your new company?" I asked.

Richard replied, "Ah Catherine! I have a job for you already. When do you want to start?"

"Tomorrow," I replied.

THE END

APPENDIX - LESSONS LEARNED SHORT STORIES

The best teacher in life is experience.

-LeBron James

Perseverance

My name is Catherine. When I graduated from university, I was passionate about starting my career journey. I started my work as an analyst in a bank. Working at the bank full time from 8 am until 2 pm every day except on Sundays. This work was not enough for me. I was hungry for knowledge and growth. I knew I could give more. So, I took a job as a lecturer in a vocational institution after my bank job, and I started teaching there from 4 pm until 8 pm. Two years later, I moved to Canada.

Finding a job in my technical domain in Quebec was a challenge. This did not stop me from learning French and finding a job. In the beginning, I took a sales job, and then one day, I received a job offer from one of the banks in Montreal. I never stopped applying to jobs in my technical field, even though at some time I felt hopeless.

Lessons Learned

Do not lose hope! Never give up trying. Eventually, you will reach your goals if you continue trying.

Enjoy your maternity or paternity leave.

Hi! My name is Susan. My first job was in sales, even though I majored in engineering. I did not give up on finding a job in my domain, and I continued searching. One day, I received an opportunity to join a bank as a developer. I was so excited to start that job that I did not take all my maternity leave, and I returned to work only after six months. In Quebec, I am allowed to take one year of paid maternity leave. Today, I regret not taking that time off because those were cherished moments with my son that I can not get back.

Lessons Learned 2:

Never give up your maternity or paternity leave for any job. Enjoy every single moment with your child counts as those memories are lost and will never come back again.

Short Story – Communicate your salary increase request to your manager

Hi! My name is Sam. One day, I discovered from chatting with the person sitting next to me that he did not have a university degree, and he got paid 10K more than me. So, I got frustrated, and someone advised me that if I get an external offer and show my manager the offer, then if they want me to stay, they can give me a counteroffer. I liked working for my company, and I wanted to increase my salary, so I played the "other offer" card. The response I got was disappointing. I was informed that there was no budget for this position. And I had been advised to accept the other position.

Lessons Learned 3:

Do not use external offers to increase your salary at your current organization. Most managers find this step intimidating. There is a high chance they will advise you to leave or take the other offer. If you want to increase your salary, simply ask your manager what you can do to increase your salary in the upcoming months. Work with your current management on a plan to increase your salary.

Short Story – Move on when your career goals are not aligned with your company's goals.

Hi! My name is John, and I am a consultant. I chose a software to be implemented in over fifty offices. I flew to the USA to be trained on this software and was responsible for its support and maintenance. While I was at this company, they hired more than 40 people as consultants to work on implementation projects related to this software. After four years at this company, I applied for a manager's position and was refused. They hired a new manager who had a master's degree in chemical engineering and without any experience in the software industry. When questioning the organization why I was not selected for this management position, they said I did not have the proper education. So, I started pursuing my master's degree after work. During this time, I got my PMP certificate, and I asked if I could have projects to handle and get the title of a project coordinator. Then, their next excuse after I had obtained my master's degree was that I did not have the proper experience.

Lessons Learned 4:

When your management does not believe in your capabilities and does not have a career plan that is aligned with your goals, it is time to move on to another job. Find the organization and the manager who believes in you and move on to evolve your skills.

Short Story – Recognition and Promotion should not be done when you submit your resignation

Hi! My name is Adam. I was hired as a project manager serving two big accounts in an IT Software company. I was given a team of 12 people to lead. Also, my responsibility was to create a master project plan for several releases. I established KPI metrics, which I shared with my management and my clients. I created a communication plan and kept upper management informed of the project updates. I received recognition for exceeding customers' expectations. This organization was awesome; we were treated as part of a family. The only problem was that after three years, I found that I was not expanding my knowledge, so I decided to take on a new and different challenge as a DevOps Manager. When I submitted my resignation, I gave my company four weeks' notice to transfer knowledge. Their response was to offer me a VP of Operations position and asked me to stay.

Lessons Learned 5:

When your company only appreciates you when you submit your resignation and give you a promotion, my advice to you is not to accept. They should have recognized and promoted you while you were growing at that organization, not when you decided to leave.

Short Story - Build leaders along as you move on your journey towards success

Hi! It is Susan again! I was working in a great engineering company where my skills were recognized and I was appreciated. I found out that one of my team members was bored with doing the same work for three years and wanted new challenges. That person was on depression medication because he was not happy at work. He was a victim of his own success. Since he did his job so well, he was stuck doing this kind of work for many years. So, I gave him new projects and he was able to deliver all of them successfully. I even mentored him on leading projects. Today, he is a successful project manager and bought his own house.

Lessons Learned 6:

Every opportunity that is given to you to help others progress, collaborate and succeed, do not miss it. Try to listen to your colleagues and to your management to better understand the objectives. Build leaders along as you move on your journey towards success.

All those good deeds will come back to you one day.

Short Story – Do not stop learning.

It is John! Given the fast-paced growth of technology, I knew that I needed to stay competitive in the market. I focused on building myself a unique job profile. I learned about different technologies, either by obtaining certifications or by working on a specific technology. I started my career in software engineering, and then I moved to project management. With the evolution of Cloud, I was interested in hardware management. Also, I wanted to know about the databases, DevOps, Security, Service Management, Process Improvement, etc.

Lessons Learned 7

Get out of your comfort zone and obtain different knowledge, diplomas, and languages. Do not stop learning! I predict that the job market will be opened for remote work all over the world. So, what makes you different than

other candidates? Why should a company hire you, not other people?

Short Story – Do not lose your health or life to work.

Hi! It is Catherine again! I am always searching for a job that gives me a work-life balance and that is challenging at the same time. In one of the positions that I held, I was given the opportunity to handle the infrastructure team, software team leads and business analysts. I was supervising around 40 employees directly. I was happy to make a positive impact, but I was working around 20 hours a day and on weekends as well. I understand that there are jobs where you work extra hours at certain times but not constant peeks. In this job, I felt like I was on a treadmill running, and it would not stop. We could not even take our vacation days due to the quantity of work that we had. I have requested more staff and help from upper management. Unfortunately, that was not possible. Day after day, I felt I was becoming unhappy. I was becoming emotionally sensitive. My tolerance and patience were degrading. I could not sleep at night and above all, I was not spending any time with my family. This is when I knew I had to move on.

Lessons Learned 8:

The true measure of success is what you have to lose to become successful. Try to understand this quote. This means that if you lose your health or your kids become drug addicts while you are working 24/7 to become a CEO, you are not successful. If your company does not accommodate you and get you the supporting staff, then you must move on and change your job. If you end up going to the hospital because of working too many hours, what will your company do for you? Think about it. Your health and family should come first.

SUMMARY

Catherine Saab is a young, dedicated, hard-working IT Operations manager who received an offer to start in her dream company called CRN Design Canada. She was promised a work-life balance, equality or women, and every Friday afternoon off in the new job. However, she ended up working on weekends and could not take her vacation days. We see throughout the story that this work was affecting her personal life and her health as well. Catherine coached her team members, led three different teams, and brought new ideas to the company. She thought she was impacting the company positively, only to find out that the global management team had a hidden agenda. Throughout the story, Catherine introduces examples of Six Sigma, Lean, ITIL, Scrum, Kanban, and Security.

ABOUT THE AUTHOR

Anastral Rusten is an IT professional leader with diverse experience in development, cloud computing, DevOps, software engineering, ITSM, and infrastructure management. She aims at aligning IT with the business. She creates strategies, develops new products, and implements smart technologies.

Anastral enjoys mentoring and coaching students. She encourages young women to get into STEM careers by guiding and sharing her experience with them. She is a positive influencer who likes to help others evolve their skills. She has compassion, passion, and perseverance to overcome hardships.

During her free time, Anastral likes to write fiction novels and read books.

Printed in the USA
CPSIA information can be obtained
at www.ICGtesting.com
LVHW060626280324
775709LV00006B/23

9 781917 007603